Kangaroo's Cancan Café

For all my friends in Australia - J.J.

For Talia and Melissa - L.C.

ORCHARD BOOKS
96 Leonard Street, London EC2A 4XD
Orchard Books Australia
32/45-51 Huntley Street, Alexandria, NSW 2015
First published in Great Britain in 2004
First paperback publication in 2005
ISBN 1 84362 354 4 (hardback)
ISBN 1 84362 600 4 (paperback)
Text © Julia Jarman 2004
Illustrations © Lynne Chapman 2004
The right of Julia Jarman to be identified as the author and of Lynne Chapman to be identified as the illustrator
of this work has been asserted by them in accordance with the Copyright, Designs and Patents Act, 1988.
A CIP catalogue record for this book is available from the British Library.
(hardback) 10 9 8 7 6 5 4 3 2
(paperback) 10 9 8 7 6 5 4 3
Printed in Singapore

Kangaroo's Cancan Café

by Julia Jarman
Illustrated by Lynne Chapman

ORCHARD BOOKS

Kangaroo went to France
And saw a great dance.
He soon became a big fan!

He sat every day
In a glitzy café,
Enjoying the jolly cancan!

But back in Australia,
With all his regalia,
His spirits started to droop.

ROO TUNES

ADVANCED HOPPING

CAMPFIRE TALES OF THE OUTBACK

Bouncy Poems

PARIS

I ♥ PARIS

He so missed the dance
That he loved in belle France,
Till he thought, "I'll start my OWN troupe!"

"I'll hold an audition!
A cancan competition!
Long-legged dancers I'll seek.

GRAND
CANCAN
COMPETITION

Auditions Today

"I'll have a Cancan Café!
Folk will come all the way
From Lilli Pilli to Albany Creek."

GRAND
CANCAN
COMPETITION
AuditionsTo

The first to turn up
Was a **wombat** called Whup.
"I don't think so," said Kanga to him.

Then a **pot-bellied pig** did a bit of a jig,
But his trotters were short – and too thin.

A dozy possum called Clive

Was the next to arrive.

"The cancan," said Kanga, "is quick!"

Z
Z
Z
z

Then a proud platypus
Caused such a big fuss,
But she didn't manage one kick.

Kangaroo, in despair,
Threw his hands in the air,
Though a **long-legged frog** was quite able.

But she lacked the height –
   And fled with stage fright
When Croc cried, "Here, dance on my table!"

Then **Croc** tried to step it.

Kangaroo said,
"Forget it.

Your cancan isn't
even so-so.

You're like all the others,
You slither and sluther;
Your bottom is much, much too low!"

Koala sleepily slurred,
"I have heard of a bird
With long legs and a bottom that's high."

Kookaburra scoffed, "Why!
That bird is too shy.
She won't dance.
She can't even fly!"

Kookaburra was right,
Emu kept out of sight,
Away from the other birds' jeers.

But Kangaroo asked politely
And she blushed very brightly –
Then she kicked ... and he broke into cheers!

As Emu kicked her legs high,
She caught Kanga's eye –
He was smit from the very first glance.

Her cancan was bliss;
He blew her a kiss,
"Emu, you really can dance!"

"Have you got emu friends?"
Kanga said at the end.
"You're fantastic!" he cried, with a whoop!

She was off with a whoosh,

"I'll ask round the bush."

And soon...

... she was back with her own cancan troupe!

GRAND
OPENING
NIGHT

Tonight!

Crowds came early and bright
For the opening night
Of Kanga's great Cancan Café.

They all sat in suspense,
  "When will it commence,
  The world-famous cancan display?"

Then into the light,
Stepped a bird bold and bright –
For Emu was no longer shy!

At the head of her clan, she began to cancan...

And the claps and the

cheers reached the sky!

The End